HOW TO STRESS FREE WITH YOGA ?

S PERUMAL

RIGI PUBLICATION

HOW TO STRESS FREE WITH YOGA ?

BY

S PERUMAL

Originally published in India

ISBN: 978-93-86447-67-8

Published by RIGI PUBLICATION

777, Street no.9, Krishna Nagar
Khanna-141401 (Punjab), India
Website: www.rigipublication.com
Email: info@rigipublication.com
Phone: +91-9357710014, +91-9465468291

PREFACE

This book pertains to the hassle-free mind. It shows you the path to obtain stable and steady mind. Through Asanas and pranayam one could get hale and healthy life. This book tells how to cope up with mental illness. With this book you could acquire more knowledge.

WHAT IS MIND?

Mind cannot be seen or touched. But it rules our actions and is responsible for the words that we speak.

The mind entertains the thoughts of desire, anger, greed, pride, jealousy and so on. Along with this positive emotions are also generated by the mind in our day to day life or social life.

During negative emotions, a lot of energy is wasted and this affects our physical and mental health.

If self-resistance is practiced, tremendous power will be manifested within.

The mind should be pure. Without pure thoughts, we cannot sleep peacefully.

To be pure, the mind should be healthy. Mental health means ability to judge reality accurately- the ability to love.

Please understand stress

A lack of mental and physical well- being caused by bitter circumstances or stipulate not in our control. There is a close relationship between mind and body.

If our mind is affected our physical body is also adversely affected.

Our mind reacts with jealously envy, hatred, fear, weariness, paleness, depression and panic. These emotions must be prevented. If we can prevent these emotions we experience a great physical and mental stress.

Sometimes, stress paves the way for heart attacks and strokes.

Worry also causes stress. This is a mental apprehension. Stress can be caused by pleasant situations as well.

Some consider stress is a typical malady of our modern world. But it existed prehistoric times as well.

Both body and mind are animated by the spirit, which has the power to heal any disease.

In yoga the process of healing involves the mind and the body.

Modern English medicine give only temporary relief and they cause new diseases due to side effects.

But in yoga there are no side effects. As far as patients are concerned, do not practice without the advice of a yogic expert.

Yoga cures life-style diseases such as diabetes, hypertension, heart disease, acidity, migraine etc.

We must know about our mind medicine. For instance, your thoughts and emotions instantly translate into alterations in brain chemistry, which, in turn affect your nervous controls, hormones and immune system.

Negativity maims while positive thoughts enhances your wellbeing and ability to fight diseases. Yoga decreases mental and emotional negativity and increases positive thoughts through Pranayama practice.

Sometimes stress gives the way ... [illegible] ... and strokes.

Worry has become ... [illegible] ... is a mental apprehension ... [illegible] ... expected or unpleasant situations ... [illegible]

Some consider ... [illegible] ... typical malady of our modern world ... [illegible]

Both body and mind are ... [illegible] ... by a spirit, which has the power to heal any disease.

[illegible] ... process of healing ... [illegible] ... the body.

[illegible]

[illegible]

[illegible]

[illegible]

[illegible] ... to fight diseases ... [illegible] ... and ... [illegible]

INDEX

MENTAL DISEASES

There are two mental diseases:

1. Psychosis

2. Psychoneurosis

Psychosis:-

This type of illness occurs of due to profound changes in mood while feeling depressed or discouraged. And they think themselves worthless. These diseases commonly known as depression.

Abnormal cheerfulness, out of keeping with reality, usually accompanied by difficulty in maintaining a consecutive conversation and inability to follow through on plan, with consequent unproductiveness.

This form of major mental illness may show symptoms as the holding of eyes which are contrary to facts (delusion), seeing things which are not present (hallucinations).

Such persons have lost touch with reality, live in the world of their own, do not see things as most people see them.

Psychoneurosis:-

It is the common problem found among all. To some extent all of us one time or another suffers from it. It is just nervousness, a sense of being fearful and depressed about the problems we face in life. If it is continued, it may be called an illness.

This illness is seen as anxiety or tension and undefined sense of worry and apprehension and sometimes followed by physical problems such as trembling sleeplessness, headache and upset stomach this is state of anxiety.

Since anxiety is the most intolerable of all sensations some mentally ill persons develop physical impairment in its place such persons are said to suffer from hysteria.

Character disorders

The forms of mental illness that most people find it difficult to accept as illness belong to the group called character disorders these are actually personality disturbances abnormal angry and aggressive deviation from normal sexual patterns, unsocial, excessive use of alcohol permanent addict to drugs.

Such people in general are characterized by a repetitive sort of self-defeating behavior, by an ability to learn experience and by being incapable of conforming to the ordinary rules of society.

We find it hard to accept them as because are we considering them as lacking in will power, moral judgement, and strength of characters.

They are unable to get along with their fellow human beings. Their characters and their personalities have been shaped by their psychological problems.

STRESS AND HYPERTENSION

High blood pressure affects millions of people. It paves the way for strokes, heart disease and kidney failure. It is called the silent killer because it has no apparent symptoms. Many people are unaware of it and go untreated.

Our heart beats 72 times a minute. Over 1,00.000 times in a single day. With every beat 70cc of blood about a half a cup is pumped in the arteries and then travels 120,00 vessels of the body. To maintain this flow of blood through the arteries there must be a driving force-the blood pressure pumped blood, exerting pressure on the walls of the arteries that is nearest to the heart and reduces as it reaches the veins.

The heart pumps blood intermittently is surges, resulting in difference of pressure during each beat.

Relaxing techniques have been considered as a potential weapon in the war on hypertension, stress management, may reduce hyper tension.

Types of Hypertension

There are two different varieties in Hypertension

1. Primacy Hypertension
2. Secondary Hypertension

Primary Hypertension:-

Majority of victims of hypertension had not reviled any proper reason but It is caused by hereditary or environment. Mostly, environment plays vital role. The killer initially manifests by a symptomless raised blood pressure.

It's victim is hale and healthy but sooner or later vital organs are affected.

Secondary Hypertension:-

A few victims here has blood pressure is completely restored to normal. In these cases damaged kidney or kidney stone our enlarged aorta, certain tumors of the glands like pituitary.

Banish High Blood Pressure to avoid hypertension

1. If overweight reduce weight to normal

2. Reducing intake of salt

3. Quit smoking

4. Quit liquor consuming

5. Break your day

6. Enjoy your work

7. Cast off despair

Depression

Depression is an illness like any other and doesn't mean that you are lazy or mad. It is all to do with chemicals in the brain and is not any one's fault.

The are two categorized depression

1. Reactive depression

2. Endogenous depression

1. Reactive depression (Exogenous depression):

This is also called exogenous depression this is a reaction to environmental stress. Sudden changes in environmental activities.

1. Job requirements
2. Death of relations
3. Accident
4. Financial loss

2. Endogenous depression:

This occurs without apparent reason. Some of them are mentioned here:

1. Inferiority complex
2. Blaming Self
3. Finding fault himself

SYMPTOMS OF STRESS

Stress cannot be found out easily. You may not be aware of it.

There are many symptoms of stress. One cannot find out rightly and specify all the symptoms. Some of them are:

1. Lack of sleep

2. Fatigue

3. Getting angry for petty reasons

4. Restlessness

5. Non consistency

6. Memory loss

7. Mood of solitude

8. Lack of concentration

9. Loss of appetite

Lack of sleep

In this world, good sleep is a medicine for all diseases. But we cannot buy good sleep. Sound sleep can be got only through a contented life. In medical shops sleeping pills are available but they can only give temporary relief. If used habitually it affects the nervous system.

During stress, rejuvenation is never felt. We may go to sleep but if there is no sound sleep we cannot get fresh physically and mentally.

In addition to this, we must voluntarily welcome sleep. Even after closing our eyes in bed inconsistent thoughts run in our mind. This is also a symptom of stress.

Fatigue

There are two kinds of fatigue.

1. Mental fatigue

2. Physical fatigue

Your mind also becomes tired. When you perform your work gleefully, both your body and mind becomes very active.

Contentment (peace) activates all glands

Coordination, the body is improved

When a farmer works strenuously he feels physical tiredness. Automatically his mind also becomes tired. This cannot be avoided. During that time you cannot think about anything.

Restlessness

Healthy living is not a problem until there is a disturbance in the natural process of sleep. In this modern world we don't have time to take rest. Private companies force us to work overtime. One can work for 8 hours a day. But if we work beyond the limit our system will eventually collapse.

The shift system of work these days is unnatural. One cannot feel refreshed even after sleeping for 10 hours in a stretch. The normal day shift work is alright. But when we work in night shifts our body becomes confused. This is because; our sleeping and eating habits change due to the shifts.

With simple techniques one can face the problem easily. The mental blocks can be overcome. Be quiet for a few seconds and think about the reasons for your stress. Subsequently you will find the answer. The reason that one finds will help to pacify the bewilderment. Some other methods can also be applied.

Kapalbhati works wonders in this regard. When we are under stress we often get very angry. Kapalbhati helps us to relieve our system from the stress knot.

Do ten Kapalbhati Pranayama without making any noise through the nostrils. This may be practiced whenever one feels stressed.

Despite over hectic schedule we must learn to relax through Shanthi Asana (See Shanthi Asana). Much energy can be got from this asana.

Restlessness will cause the person to lose their composure with those who talk with them. They cannot answer even simple questions. They would look lazy and inactive.

People who are working as managers in large companies should relax themselves at least half an hour a day through yoga.

Non consistency

One cannot lead a successful life with an unstable mind. An unstable mind changes thoughts without any proper reason or proper decision.

Proper Attention

If you decide to go to the market, your thoughts must be about the market. But an unstable mind jumps from one thing to another. This has to be stopped. Otherwise, your goals cannot be achieved.

Along with this, often forgetfulness is also a sign of stress.

One can converse with others for more than a hour. In between, some thoughts and facts are forgotten. And at once, one could go back what he had thought of. Again, one must begin from cut thought words.

All these could be managed by relaxation and a pacified manner.

Getting angry for petty reasons:

All are vulnerable to emotions. Our mind is caught in some feelings which cannot be freed easily. Our mind is restless in thoughts. Forever thoughts are flowing. One cannot stop it.

When good things happen our psyche dwells in pleasant palace. And at a time when worry or any other negative emotions imprisoned the mind, circumstances might disturb us in many ways- sometimes, sudden anger is possible.

In this fast world men and women have to adjust with time.

Incapability of time management leads to unwanted conflicts.

For example, you have to be by 9.00 am at the office. But daily you reached at 9:10 or 9:20. Then your boss will get angry with you and shows remorse.

Along with this, at your home, every morning while leaving for office you are in a hurry. During that time, if anyone of your family asks you to help you become bewildered.

When we are affected with stress, our mind and thoughts are easily caught in bewilderment. And unable to tolerate this we burst out at even for no reason or for petty reason.

STRESS TOWARDS PROGRESS

Change is vital. So, stress is inevitable. It should be managed.

When change is occurred, there will be negative and positive results. During that time we need an adaptation.

We are living in 21st century. All science has progressed. Adaptation requires effort. As we are in society, we are in great flux. Rapidly, adapting at many different levels simultaneously, Knowledge broadens. Knowledge become realities. That we must deal with.

So, speed of progress is stress that is going towards change. Rate of change is always with overload. Overload leads to stress. It should be managed.

New research – "*Right is not okay*"

It is one of the most natural actions in the world - A mother scoops up a baby to hold and comfort it in her arms. But according to new research, cradling could help identify stress that may lead to postnatal depression. New mothers who cradle their infants on the right side of their body may be displaying signs of 'extreme stress'. The findings built on previous research showing that most mothers prefer to hold their baby to their left, regardless of whether they are left or right handed.

The latest study suggests there is a correlation between the minority which holds a baby on the right and a greater likelihood that they are experiencing stress beyond levels natural in new parents. The researchers say the finding could provide a new way to address postnatal depression. They conclude 'Studying no-verbal eves such as baby cradling could help doctors and health visitors identify which mother needs extra professional support.'

Depression in mothers can have a detrimental effect on the baby's mental development.

Mothers were asked to cradle their babies, and action which, the research established was not linked to left or right handedness.

They are also quizzed on their mental- state.

WORK LIFE BALANCE

In our life work is essential. Without work, human can be boring.

Work - life- health = balance.

All these are interlinked. One can lead a successful life while work and health are not considered.

A devoted work provides us a peaceful day. One has to enjoy the job that one is doing.

Primarily we have to look at life-our ambitions drive our education and leisure activity.

It is a well-known fact that most teenagers do not have a daily routine to maintain health.

They go for a job as early as possible. They want to earn more. They do not want to wait. Thus they lose their peace. They think that earning money is life. It is only a part of our life. They want to go to greater heights. And at the same time the pressure nears its zenith.

Work in the office seems unending. Demands in home and family reach new heights. Words like time management, de stressing, quality time are often repeated. This situation is common to most of the work force globally. They are not restricted to one country or region.

People are thinking that today's life is as never before. Stress increased in maintaining good individual health to cope up with new pressures in the work place.

In the whole world, meditation and asanas are widely practiced. They are needed to re-energize, maintain composure throughout the day, to unwind and to relax at the end of the day.

People are following several methods of fitness, relaxation and exercise techniques. But yoga plays a vital role in dealing with all kinds of physical and mental need of human beings.

FAMILY AND DE STRESSING

Couples across the globe are sharing house hold chores to save time. Working mothers in the US are now opting to work part time rather than full time.

In India, in most of the families, mothers are not willing to work. But people in cities like Chennai, Mumbai, Delhi and Calcutta have to go to work to make both ends meet. Single earning leads to economic problem. Double earning is the only option.

Parents get up together as early as possible and they work together to prepare Breakfast, lunch and they prepare their children for school. This makes them reach the peak of their stress.

Till the return of the parents the children have to stand outside. Many after school care centers have been opened in the cities. They have to wait till 6 or 7 pm. Then the parents come and take them home.

It is very pathetic to see parents having no time to look after their children and to be kind to them. If the children demanded attention, the parents would become frustrated due to lack of time. During Sundays, they have time to relax. Many consider week days are hell but holidays not heaven.

DIET AND STRESS

We may infer what the relationship between diet and stress is. But they are closely interlocked.

Both cannot be separated. Bad food would increase stress. The digestive system will be affected.

We should feel comfortable physically at any time for which we have to put a few rules and regulations in our daily diet chart. Before that, let us know about our digestive system, how it works, how it eliminates the wastages.

If you want to be mentally and physically active, you cannot afford to overload your digestive system.

Heavy food, high protein food leads you to the ladder of laziness.

Your stomach needs more blood when, the blood to brain is slightly cut off.

Excessive intake of proteins leads you to coronary heart disease. By products are toxins and it causes ulcer.

Cats, Dogs, Lions and tigers are carnivores. Cows, Sheep and Goats are herbivorous.

Pure carnivores have a high concentration of hydrochloric acid in their stomach. They have a very short intestine. These quickly break down into protein, and the excretion comes out quickly.

The acid in human stomach is weaker than the acid of pure carnivores and the intestines are larger for the digestion of carbohydrates.

Excess protein leads to maintenance of muscular tension. This would eventually damage our heart. Amino acid tyrosine creates Adrenaline known as stress hormone). This is because of eating meat.

Meat- Amino acid- Adrenaline

Vegetarians – Tryptophane – Serotonin (relaxation chemical)

If you take vegetables, the Tryptophane creates Serotonin is surplus.

If you take more protein, there is a need of more acid to break it down.

FRUITS AND STRESS

Hypertension, stress and depression are mind related diseases. We can recover from them by taking more fruit juices.

Fruits are a natural way to good health. Fruits and vegetables can cure many serious diseases.

These are good for health and vitality.

Fruits contain pure water, sugar, vitamins, minerals, alkali, organic acids, proteins, fat and fibre.

Asthma, chronic cold, bronchitis, jaundice and kidney diseases can be cured easily because fruits are alkaline in nature.

We should consume raw fruit without adding any spices. To reduce high blood pressure and stress, we can eat pomegranate, papaya, orange and lemon. For low pressure, mosambi, carrot can be taken.

Garlic can bring down blood pressure and stress. Garlic has heating and drying properties. Its juice is a disinfectant, rejuvenate and antispasmodic.

Garlic is also found effective in relieving joint pains and arthritis.

IMPORTANT METHODS TO BEAT STRESS

Stress always outward meditation which means concentrating the objects or things with open eyes.

While practicing outward meditation, accumulated fear and feelings will be released and the mind will become empty and will be de stressed.

Those who are affected by severe stress related problems like neck pain, head ache have outward meditation.

Outward meditation leads to free flow and continuity of actions. When one is affected by severe stress, routine work is affected. As far as outward meditation is concerned staring at light is one of the best methods to tackle this problem.

Inward meditation and outward meditation

In outward meditation, two types are recommended.

1. Steady gazing at a single focal point.

2. The reflection of your own face in a mirror.

To practice both, one should consult a competent yoga instructor.

Candle meditation

The object (candle) should be at eye level.

It should be central.

It should be at arm's length.

Sit and close your eyes in a comfortable and steady position.

You maintain that posture for some time.

Be still…

After a minute, open your eyes and gaze at the tip of the wick.

It should be done with utmost relaxation.

Try to avoid forced concentration.

Avoid tense eyes.

Your thoughts should be on the flame.

Often you have to close your eyes.

After absorbing the flame, your eyes should be closed and internal relationship between flame and mind should be very strong.

Having practiced this, relax your eyes and continue to gaze.

If there are any changes in color and form consciously relax your eyes.

SHANMUKI MUDRA AND STRESS BEATING

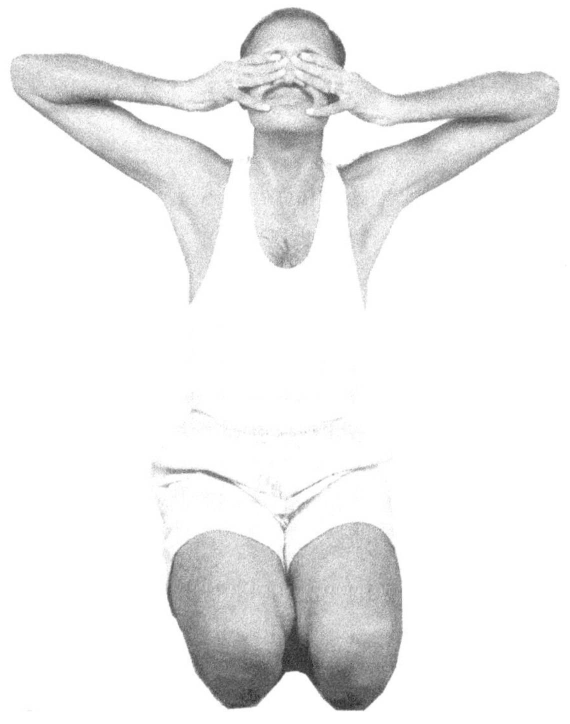

Shanmuki mudra plays a vital role in stress busting. We must understand our thoughts and feelings.

When we close our eyes our thoughts become reduced. When we totally close our eyes our mind becomes completely still.

There are five senses. Sight and hearing are crucial.

Let us discuss the method of practicing "Shanmuki Mudra".

Method:

Sit in vajrasana or in Padmasana or in suhasana posture.

The spine should be erect.

First, hold your palms as if offering prayers. And as shown in the figure, the right and left thumb close the ears, front fingers and middle fingers on closed eyes, ring finger on nose and that should not be closed.

In this posture stress comes down. Some kind of internal rhythm will be heard. One should concentrate on the inner voice. One should practice it for 10 to 15 minutes.

Through this we train our mind to be still. One will be away from this world. Connection to this world is disconnected. Many colors appear in the mind. This indicates the philosophy of panchapudha. Yogis could realize it clearly.

Elders cannot do this for more than 5 minutes. They feel pain in their hands. So they could utilize other methods to practice it.

ANEMIC AND STRESS

Anemia can also be a result of sustained emotional strain and anxiety, which affects the production of hydrochloric acid essential for the assimilation of proteins and iron.

Anemia means that the blood does not have enough hemoglobin, the oxygen carrying iron compound. It is red.

When the body does not have enough oxygen, it is unable to burn off sugar to create energy.

Iron does not produce energy but it helps in transporting of nutrients and oxygen.

Normal level of hemoglobin is 15gm per 100 cc of blood.

It is vital for respiratory and metabolic efficiency.

Poor eyesight, poor memory, general body weakness, fatigue are due to the lack of hemoglobin in the blood.

MENTAL ILLNESS AND TREATMENT

It is very difficult to find out the persons who are mentally imbalanced. Mental illness is not open for discussion. It might be due to stress also.

They often ignore tentative suggestions from close friends and they refuse to acknowledge a problem.

One should accept that body and mind complement each other. To treat mental disorder one can begin treatment from physical problem.

Many therapies are available to treat mental disorder. But among all, yoga plays a vital role in this treatment.

Introverts and those unwilling to disclose their problems to friends and family members could have anonymous blocks.

First of all, they should learn to discuss about their problems.

Talking to a friend, spouse or confidante may make Pranayama.

PRANAYAMAM

Prana -means vital force, yama -means to control. It means to control the prana, not the air. (Ordinary breathing)

Pranayamam plays a vital role in stress busting and is a direct link between "prana" and the mind-both Inseparable.

While you are under stress the number of times of taking breath will be more and the length of the breaths will be very short. When you are relaxed the breathing will be normal.

Our mind takes us into the world of unwanted things but our Prana endeavors to ramshackle from going there.

To lead this life peacefully, some power is in need for constraining our thoughts from going astray that may be from outside world.

Every individual has the power to run his own machine. The machine should have pure oil. It is easy to handle the situation.

Slough the stress

1. Surya Kalai (Surya- Sun- heat)

2. Chandra Kalai (Chandra- Cool (Moon)- Left nose)

3. Seethalai

4. Bhastrika

5. Kapalbhati

Generally one should start Pranayama with right hand. The thumb for right nose. The ring finger for left nose. Usually, breathe in only one nostril either left or right. Not in both at the same time.

This tunes up our nervous system and enhances natural immunity.

Pranayama is nothing but a vital force which regulates all system of the body to make it energetic.

According to Indian sages, rishies and monks life depends on the breathing and the length of the breaths. Through decreasing the number of breaths we can increase our life span.

1. Surya Kalai

Sit in padmasana, keep the spine now close your left nose till with right hands ring finger.

Now inhale for 5 seconds and exhale in the same nose for 10 seconds (1:2)

Do this ten times. Ratio may be increased after a month of practice.

2. Chandra Kalai

Now, close your nose with the right hand thumb. As in Suryakalai, inhale for 5 seconds and exhale for 10 seconds.

Both Suryakalai and Chandrakalai balance heat and the cold in our body.

3. Bhastrika

Inhale through both nostrils for 10 seconds and exhale for 20 seconds.

In this type no hands are used. It may be repeated 10 to 20 times a day.

4. Kapalbhati

Kapala means head

Pathi – pure

To purify the system in the head. This Pranayama may be practiced in Padmasana or in the position of laying down.

All parts of the body must be relaxed. Now exhale speedily pushing the breath forcibly through both nostrils with quick succession and should not inhale voluntarily, but a little amount of air towards lungs may be allowed.

Initially one would feel giddiness during practice but after ten days this will go. This increases the flow in the brain and the respiratory passage is cleared and Sinus and asthma related troubles will also be cured.

This gives agility and freshness to the body. If one feels headache caused by stress this will help to rejuvenate.

PADMASANA

1. Lotus pose asana

Before telling about the method of doing this asana, one should know about this posture.

Many benefits can be reaped from this asana. Generally, our health is our spine. One can be in this posture for many hours. The practitioner can attain 'perfect unity with mind and body'.

Being erect helps all glands to function effectively. No disease will attack us. Knee pain can be cured.

Initially it may be difficult to practice. But practice makes perfection. If one starts to practice as shown in the figure no difficulty will be felt by them. This asana is mostly used for meditation and practicing pranayama.

PADMASANA

1. Sit on the floor

2. Stretch both legs

3. Bend the right leg at the knee

4. With the help of hands place it at the left thigh

5. Now, bend the left leg and place it on the right thigh

6. In both the legs, the foot should be near the naval

7. In this posture, the spine should be erect

8. People, who are used to eating on the dining table, would feel difficult to practice initially.

9. Change the leg position by placing right foot over the left and the left foot over the right.

10. This asana relaxes the spine, the feet and the ankles.

11. This asana is used for practicing pranayama and meditation.

UTHITHA PADAASAN

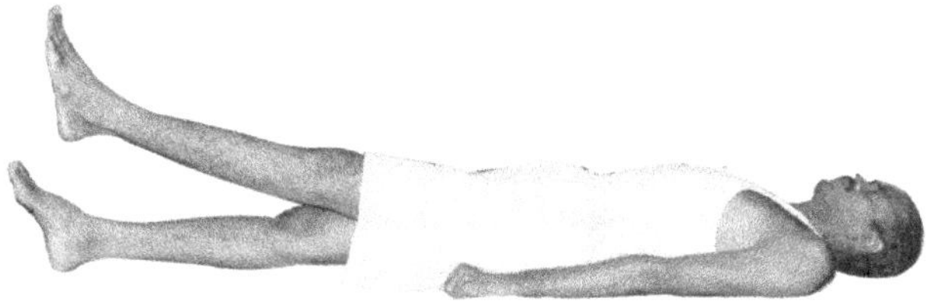

This asana can be practiced by all ages. It is very simple. It is easy to relax through this asana.

Uthitha means lift in Sanskrit. Pada means legs (feet). Both legs are to be lifted. For this artha uthitha pada asan must be practiced.

Artha means half posture. Lie down on a mat. Both hands should touch the body as shown in the figure.

Take five deep breaths.

First lift the right leg until it reaches 45 degree angle. Stay for then seconds and then relax. Take two deep breaths. Repeat this five times.

The left leg should also be practiced in the same way.

While staying on this posture, learn to relax. By this only yogic power will pass into all parts of the body.

There are many uses for this asana. Blood flow will be increased to the abdomen.

So, digestive process **PAVAMUKTHASAN.**

PAVANAMUKTHASAN

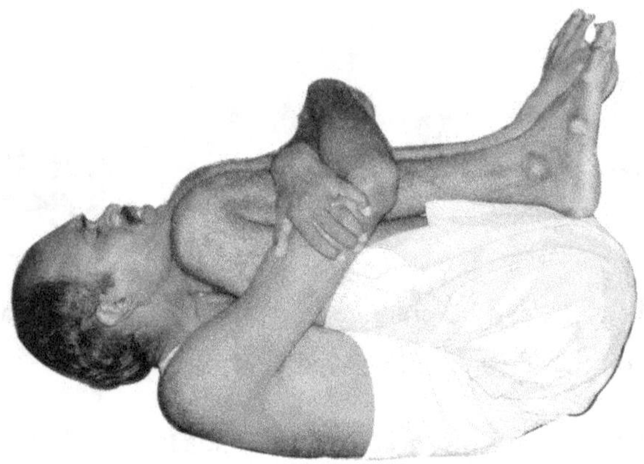

There are many types of Pavanamukthiasans. Lie down on a mat. Take five deep breaths.

Then fold your right leg. Try to touch the right knee with your chin. Stay like that for ten seconds. Then relax for a while.

Beginners should practice this as much as possible. One should not stiffen any muscle while doing asana.

This asana helps one to relax the thigh muscle. This contradicts gastric trouble. It relieves air lock in the body.

Initially one must take five seconds for doing one time. And slowly increase the duration and number of times.

Those with a large belly will feel hard to do this. They must take advice from a yogic expert and change their food habits so as to relax their nervous system and their muscles.

This helps in reducing unwanted flesh from the thighs and abdomen. This is panacea for those suffering

This seems to be very easy. But just hand to practice those who with pot like belly. They may do it as far as possible. Spread your legs as in Patchimottasana. Fold your right leg. Knees should touch the chin. Breathing is normal. Unnecessary flesh would go away. Gas trouble would be eradicated. Besides, It relaxes the knee muscles. Do it three to five times a day.

ARTHAHALAASAN

This is half of the posture of halasan. Lie on the back. Take five to ten breaths.

Now raise your legs until it reaches ninety degrees. Keep like that for ten seconds. Hold your breath and in experience try to bring back to normal breath. Now come back to first stage. This can be done 7 times a day with 10 to 15 seconds for each posture.

This has all the benefits of pavanamukthasan from muscle catch to gas trouble.

JANUSEERASAN

Janu means knee in Sanskrit. To practice this asana one has to learn Padmasana very well.

First of all, spread your right leg. The left leg should be as shown in the picture. Try to hold the right leg. Beginner may bend the knee and then may try to straight for perfect posture.

Stay in the position for 10 seconds. Repeat it four times a day. While staying in the posture, breathing should be normal.

After a month of this kind of practice, you have to touch the knee with your forehead. The position should be comfortable and relaxed.

"This asana may be recommended for eradication of kidney diseases as well as nervous disorder due to weakness and anemic".

FORWARD BENT PATCHIMOTTASANA

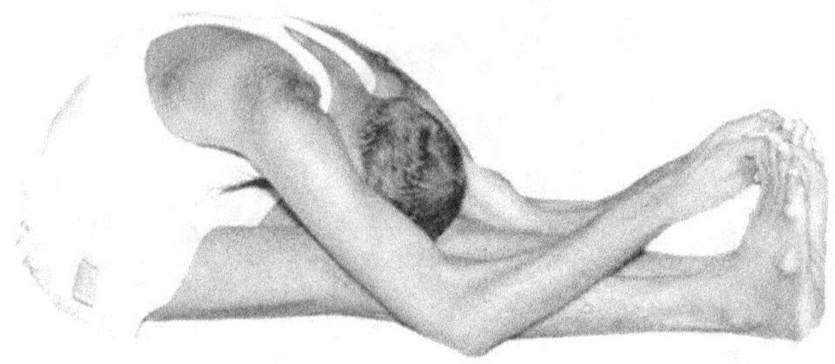

Intense stretching of back relieves stress in spinal chord. It means, all muscles feel relaxed. The stiffness is decreased.

On a psychological level, the patchmottasana is excellent for developing patience. If we get easily discouraged or unable to sustain interest for some time or simply cannot enter into long term commitments then this is an excellent position to cultivate those qualities.

The back is an indicator for the stress we endure. Stress causes disruption in relationships- both at work and home. The logical mind, though functional, leaves no room for healthy emotional expression if one does not leave about it.

Hence a survival mechanism, emotions are suppressed and stored in the back to be dealt with later. The suppressed stress, apart from causing back ache, comes out at different times as burst of anger or rage. The person may also feel depressed, which is a sign of suppressed anger or irritation. So, systematic cleaning of these emotions is needed and can be done through this asana.

When it is done with care and concentration, it releases the layers of stress that builds up in the system.

It requires regular practice and is a function of hour intensely as well as for how long the focus is directed on the back.

It makes us turn more inward.

The Technique:

Sit comfortably with your feet stretched out. Hug your thighs from below. Walk forward up to the point where your chest is still in contact with your thighs. The extent to which you will be able to bend forward will depend on the flexibility of your back and lengthen your spine. Come up gently. Hug your knees. Breathe in and stretch up. Breathe out and release.

Patchimothasan. Patchi means bird- This is called flying posture. Stretch your legs. Hold your legs as shown in the picture. This is the first step.

Then you may try to touch the knees with the forehead. Entire nervous system would be very active. Laziness will fly away. All kinds of abdominal problems would be cured. Pancreas and Kidneys would be rejuvenated. Breathing is normal. Stay in the position for ten seconds. Repeat it for three to five times daily.

"If one is suffering from back pain, one must avoid or may practice this with the help of a yogic expert"

BHUJANKASAN

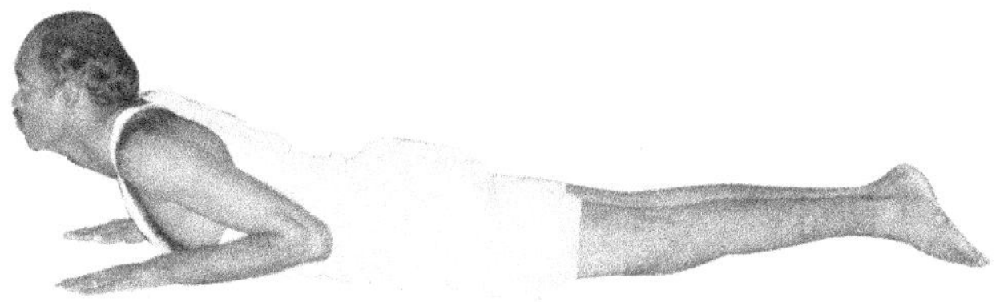

Bhuja Symbolizes snake. Snake symbolizes Kundalini- Natural power that inherited in each man and woman. The energy should be uncovered through asanas and pranayama. This is microcosm. Universe is Macro Cosm.

In this asana our internal power is brought out.

And with this, all kinds of back pain would be cured and spondylitis too.

DHANUR ASAN

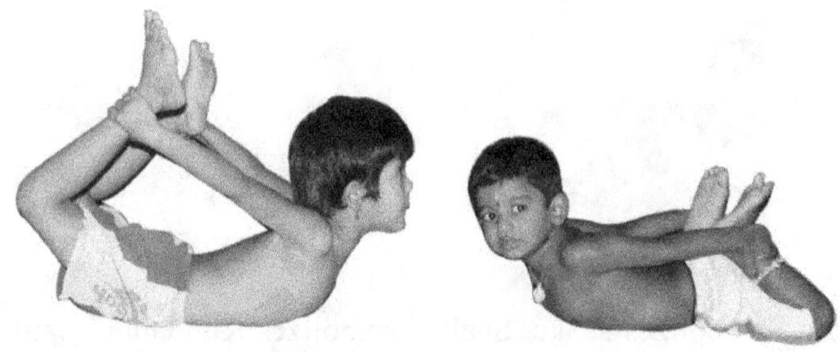

Dhanu means bow. This asana resembles bow.

One can reap more benefits through practicing this asana. Lie down as shown in the picture. Hold your right ankle with right hand so as left ankle with left leg.

Now just lift the legs as well as hands simultaneously.

your chest also would be enlarged.

In this posture, breathing should be normal. One can practice three times. Each time should not be more than 15 seconds.

SALABASAN

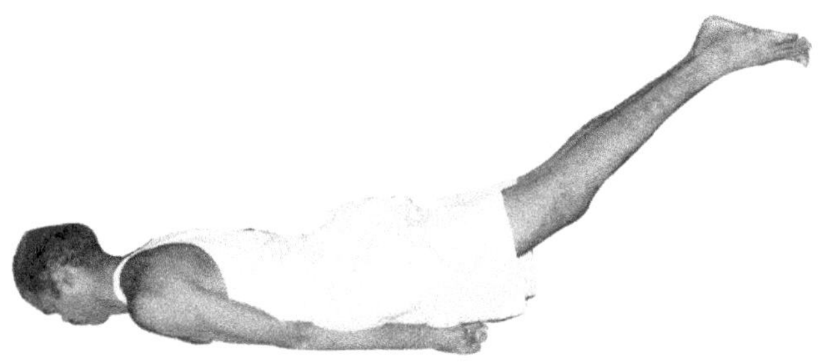

Artha means half in Sanskrit. Lie down on the mat. Both hands should be joined together. Put under the stomach. The chin should touch the floor. Hold the breath and lift your right leg as high as possible. Stay for 5 seconds in the posture and relax it. Take two deep breaths.

And alternatively, practice the left leg.

After a month, you may practice in both legs.

Abdominal problems would be cleared away and gas trouble, indigestion and impotency will also be cured.

While holding the breath, your thoughts will not be deviated. So your mind becomes still. Stress would be increased.

THRATAK

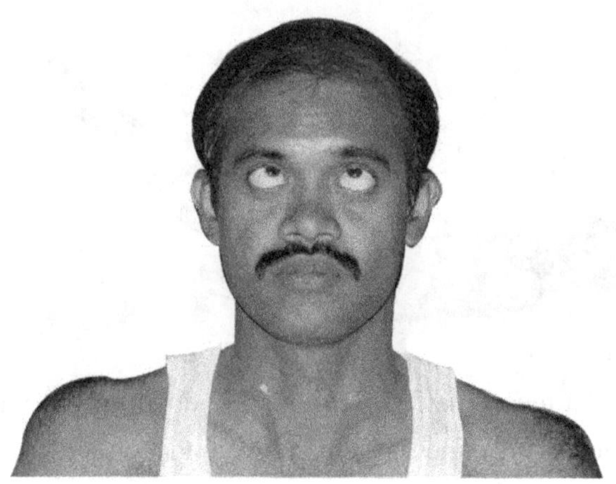

It means concentrate on one thing with eyes. Both eyes should face the center of forehead (Third eye). This is third eye. This is the place of more power. It activates 'Agna Chakra' related problems will be eradicated. It gives relaxation to the brain. Sit in Padmasana posture. Take ten deep breaths closing the eyes. In our brain is the hypothalamas, that controls our good and bad thoughts. Through thratak and sirasasana it is balanced.

NINDRAPADA ASAN

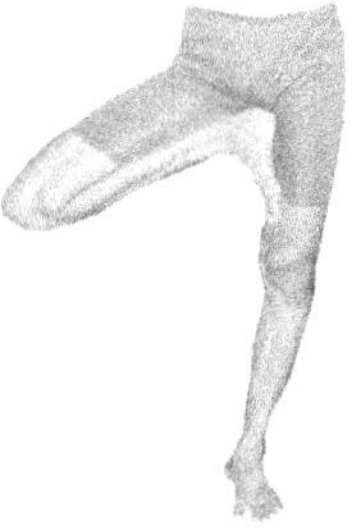

Single leg standing posture. It seems to be easy to practise. But physical and mental coordination is important.

Right leg should be on the left thigh. Hands to be over the head as in the picture. Strain in the hands should be avoided.

Stay for ten seconds in this position. To practice this asana, concentration is vital. If your thoughts are deviated, you cannot last in the position even for five seconds.

If one does it for 10 minutes a day, at a stretch, he will conquer everything in the world.

One has to go with it closing the eyes that would increase the power of intellect and consciousness.

Stress would fly away. Mental strain would also go away. This is counter pose to Arthasiras asan This asana leg stand posture brings your left foot and place. In right thigh bring your hands above head as in the posture. Stay for 10 seconds. Do it three times with alternative legs this asana helps in maintaining stability of mind and body in physical mental co-ordination. In you close your eyes in the posture you could for stay for long time.

MATHYASAN

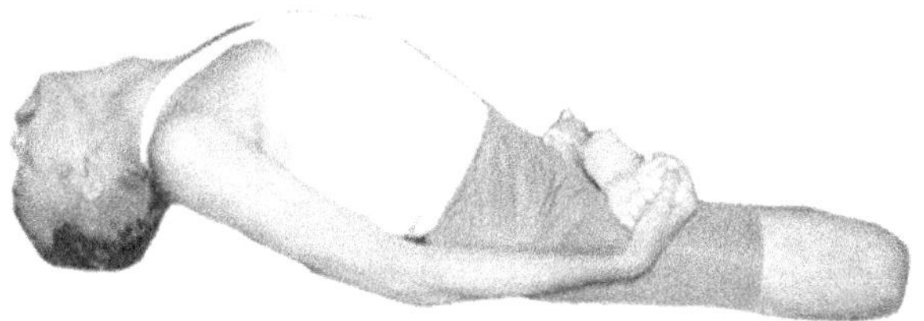

This asana resembles fish. Before reaching perfection one has to do three steps:

First sit properly with the legs stretched. Place a pillow behind the practitioner as shown in the figure.

Lie on the pillow. Waist should be under the pillow. Now take five deep breaths. Stay for ten seconds in the position. Practise it three times daily.

It relaxes the brain and the flow of blood to the brain will increase. This is due to the expansion of lungs and heart. With this kapa related diseases will be eradicated.

VAJRASANA

Vajram is a strong and mighty weapon of Lord Indira. It one practices it one will get that power.

Single fold asana

Sit on the mat. As in the picture, fold two legs and place buttocks on the ankles. Put your spinal cord erect. Place your palms on the knees.

Take 10 deep breaths- (exhale and inhale rhythmically)

Our health depends on our spinal chord. If it is kept erect, all the glands will be active. A crooked spinal cord is not good for health.

With this knee pain can be relieved. But one must practice this on the advice of a yogic expert considering the age.

In this modern life, only a few of us take food sitting on the ground. Most of us use dining table. So we lose our knee flexibility.

MAHAMUDRA

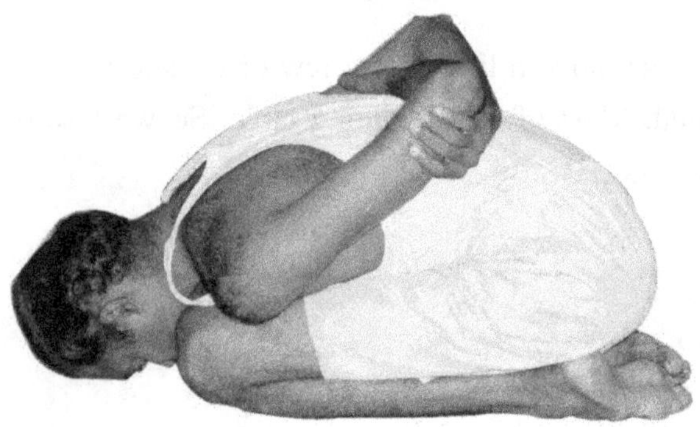

This does not come under asana. It comes under mudra. Mudra means symbols.

Sit in the Vajrasana posture. Be erect. Take five deep breaths. Join both wrists behind lower spinal cord as shown in the queue. Now bend forward. Face should touch the ground with normal breath.

Stay like that for ten seconds. There are 72,000 nervous pulses in our body. They all should be very active and through which energetic- vital prana passes.

This is three fold asana. Even though we have practiced many levels of asanas, it maintains resilience of nervous system.

Some people with a large belly cannot bend forward. They should practice 'Anga Prathatchana'. It will be comfortable to practice. Blood flow to all parts of the body will increase.

VAMAYOGAMUDRA

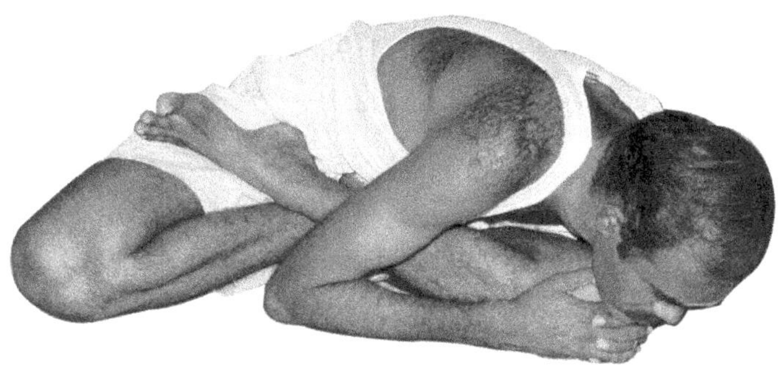

Sit comfortably in Sukasana posture or padmasana postures with both hands placed on right knee and touch the chin on the knee. Stay for ten seconds and then relax taking two deep breaths. One must practice this five to seven times.

VIBAREETHAKARANAI

Vibareethakaranai, not asana but a kind of Mudra, which keeps body and mind always fresh, through practicing daily this asana one can cure all kind of maladies.

To have seen, this is simple one. But effects copious.

In our abdomen is a natural light - its flame flows upwards that burns up all kinds of unwanted things in our digestive system.

To practice this, as shown in the picture, one could seek yogic expert's help initially until reaches perfection.

This can be done by all age groups. Anyone suffering from Blood pressure and hypertension one must do with the help of yogic expert.

Aged people can use vibareethakarani bed. One could realize 80% benefits of sarvangasan through doing this Mudra.

ARTHASIRASASAN

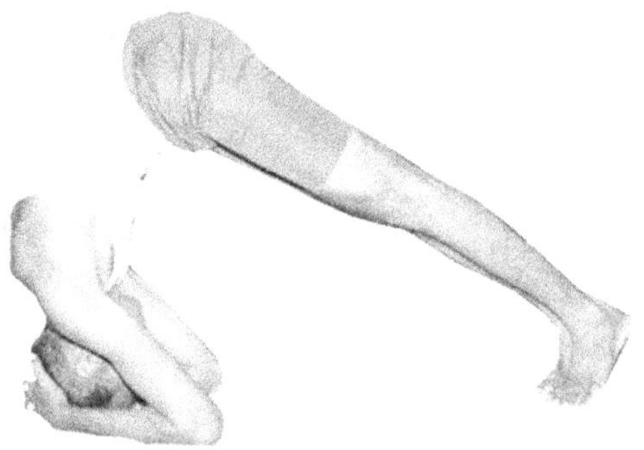

Artha - means Half, Half posture of sirasasan.

Doing Mahamudha bring your hands as shown in the picture (interlocking fingers) Put your legs as hear as possible while practicing the asana, keep your eyes closed. Normal breathing. Stay for 20 seconds, practice it three times a day. And in second month stay for 30 seconds a time.

While you release, your should not lift your head atonce. But come to Mahamudra Position and then lift your head and come to normal position.

SARVANGASAN

Sarvam - all, Asanam - Posture

All kinds of parts of body gets more uses through this asana. Top to bottom all organs would be very active.

Actually it is a shoulder stand Anyone suffering from back pain shoulder pain and spondylitis should not practice it.

Lie down on the mat. Do arthahalasan at once. lift your legs as shown in the picture initially for few days, one could not reach the full posture. Stay for 10 seconds practice it 5 times a day. After a month of practice, increase the duration till 3 minutes at a stretch.

HALASAN

Halasan means plough posture. Practice Sarvangasana, and bring your legs down as snown in the picture.

Stay for 10 seconds in the position and do 5 times a day. After a week of practice increase the duration till 15 seconds per time.

Day by day, the perfection can be reached. This asana can cure all kind of diseases relating to lungs sinusitis would be eradicated. Nose blockage too.

SHANTHI ASANA

1. Lie down on the floor.

2. Spread your legs and hands as in the picture.

3. Half closed eyes.

4. Think upon every parts of the body.

5. Stay for 10 minutes in the position in awaken state.

6. Don't sleep.

MARJARI ASANA

This asana released the spine. It prevents one from disc prolapse and all kinds of glands just near to spinal chord would be active while practicing this asana.

First kneel down. Come to the position as in the picture that place your parallel and the distance between the hands should be one feet and the distance between the hands and legs not less than one and a half feet.

Now, lift your head above, eyes should look upwards, simultaneously waist be bent downwards as far as possible. During this time, breathing should be normal. Stay for 10 seconds. And again bring your waist as crooked as possible at the same time bring your head inwards as far as possible. Stay for 10 seconds. Repeat it 10 times days.

OBSESSIVE COMPULSIVE DISORDER AND STRESS (OCD)

Obsessive compulsive Disorder is a serious anxiety related condition.

It affects from young children to older adults- regardless of gender and social or cultural background.

It is because of the intense feelings of embarrassment, guilt and sometimes even shame associated with what is often called the 'Secret Illness'.

Here, stress and OCD has a clear link.

In times of stress, OCD symptoms are experienced.

The illness can have a totally devastating effect on work, social life and personal relationships.

OCD can take many forms, sufferers experience repetitive, intrusive and unwelcome thoughts, images, impulses and doubts which they could not ignore.

These thoughts do not appear in mind always.

These thoughts form the obsessional.

Part of Obsessive Compulsive Disorder

Sufferers try to fight these thoughts with mental or physical rituals, the compulsions, which involve repeatedly by performing actions such as washing, cleaning, checking, counting, hoarding or part taking in endless rumination.

However, this often results in further worrying and preoccupation with the obsessional thoughts.

Most sufferers know that their thoughts and behavior are irrational and senseless but incapable of stopping them. This has a significant impact on their confidence and self-esteem and a result, their careers, relationships and lifestyles.

To sufferers and non- sufferers alike, thoughts and fears related to OCD can seem profoundly shocking.

It would be fair to say that most individuals at some stage in their lives, have come into contact with the phenomenon of obsessional or intrusive thinking and or succumbed to the seemingly non sensual need to perform an odd and often unrelated behavior pattern in order to avert a real or imagined danger, e.g. toweling a certain them of furniture before going to bed in order to ward off nightmare or checking several times that the door and windows are locked before leaving the house when going on holiday.

Compulsions or compulsive acts can be defined as repetitious, purposeful actions in which the individual feels compelled to engage according to their own rules or in a stereo typed manner.

The individual experiences a sense of resistance to the act but this is overridden by the strong, subjective drive to perform the action. Most often the principal aim behind the compulsive act is to generate temporary relief from the anxiety compulsions can be covered.

More about OCD:

We have to recognize obsessive thoughts and compulsive urges and should understand it.

It is important to increase our mindful awareness that these intrusive thoughts and urges are symptoms of a medical disorder.

Recent scientific research on OCD has found that by leasing to resist obsessions and compulsions through behavior therapy. You can actually change the biochemistry that is causing the OCD symptoms. Through Yoga's one can recover. Yoga works wonders in this regard. That only can be experienced. I cannot explain. Some realizations cannot be illustrated.

OCD cannot be eradicated in seconds or minutes.

That process of changing the underlying biological problem. It may take weeks or even months. It requires patience and persistent effort.

Yoga treatment is behavioral treatment- that is to respond to the thoughts and urges are within our control. No matter how strong and bothersome that may be. The goal is to control our responses to the thoughts and urges not to control the thoughts and urges themselves to resist them.

Deep inside the brain lies a structure called the caudate nucleus. Scientists worldwide have studied this structure and believe that, in people with OCD, the caudate nucleus may be malfunctioning. Think of the caudate nucleus as a processing center or filtering station for the very complicated messages generated by the front part of the brain, which is probably the part used in thinking, planning and understanding. Together with its sister structure, the putamen, which is next to it, the caudate nucleus functions like an automatic transmission in a car. The caudate nucleus and putamen which together are called the striatum take in messages from very complicated parts of the brain- those that control body movement, physical feelings. They function in unison like an automatic transmission, assuming the smooth transition from one behavior to another. Typically when anyone decides to make a movement, intruding movement and misdirected feelings are filtered out automatically. So that the desired movement can be performed rapidly and efficiently. There is a quick, smooth shifting of gears.

During normal day, we make many rapid shifts of behavior, smooth and easily and usually without thinking about them. It is the functioning of the caudate nucleus and putamen that makes this possible. In OCD, the problem seems to be that smooth, efficient filtering and the shifting of thoughts and behavior are disrupted by a shifter in the caudate nucleus.

As a result of malfunction, the front of the brain becomes overactive and uses excessive energy. It is like you are struck in a ditch. You spin, spin and spin on your wheels.

Positive Outlook:

Our views and thoughts lead stress. We shall have to learn good things in everything and learn to think positively.

Optimist spends his day happily. Pessimist mind works against it.

Even though, in our day to day life, negative and positive dealings are casual, we must hope for positive look but prepare for negativity.

Obsessive Compulsive Disorder and Stress (OCD)

Obsessive Compulsive Disorder is a serious anxiety - related condition.

It affects from young children to older adults - regardless of gender and social and cultural background. It is because of the intense feelings of embarrassment, guilt and sometimes even shame associated with what is often called the 'secret illness'.

Here, stress and OCD has a clear link. In times of stress, OCD symptoms are experienced.

The illness can have a totally devastating effect on work, social life and personal relationships.

OCD can take many forms, sufferers experience repetitive, intrusive and unwelcome thoughts, images, impulses and doubts which they could not ignore.

These thoughts do not appear in mind always. These thoughts form the obsessional part of obsessive compulsive disorder.

Yoga Treatment for O.C.D.

Follow the week wise course as in the program.

MORE ABOUT STRESS

Muscles relaxation is stress relief:

There is a close relationship between mind and muscle. Those with stiff muscles are vulnerable to sudden anger.

When you relax your muscle your mind and thoughts become automatically relaxed. Residence of the muscle determines our happiness and relaxation. It leads to peace.

Eyes and distressing

Palm:

Rub your hands together briskly for 20 seconds or so, then cup your palms over your eyes without applying any pressure.

Tip:

If you use a computer, rest your eyes by palming for at least one minute for every 15 minutes. You estimate you are looking at the screen while palming try to recall an object in the brightest possible colors.

Blinking:

Do that for 10 to 20 seconds, several times a day, as you do, turn your head gently from left to right and back again.

Splashing:

Gently splash warm water over your closed eyes 20 times, then repeat 20 times with cold water to improve circulation to the eyes.

Diet and stress:

What you eat also helps to bring down your stress levels.

Drink more water:

By drinking plenty of water we can prevent stress. Drinking six to ten glasses of water a day is essential. This would be very helpful for all chemical reactions in the body.

More fruits:

Fruits and vegetables contain more phyto- chemicals. This prevents cancer and heart disease.

Varied vegetables:

Vegetables, dried peas, beans, lentils and fruits provide some starch and low amount of sugar, vitamins, minerals and dietary fiber. Vegetables and fruit are high in antioxidants, vitamin C and beta carotene which the body can turn into vitamin A.

Sleeping

Eat to sleep

An amino acid called frypan, found in milk, peanuts helps the brain to produce serotonin, a chemical that helps you to relax.

Check your Iron levels: Iron deficient women are 20 percent more likely to sleep badly.

Try nature's sleep aids:

Try homoeopathic remedies to insomnia.

Create a sleep sanctuary.

Stop watching the idiot box. Don't read anything that is work related. If you wake up, don't turn on the light.

Avoid these foods:

Oil, butter, table, margarine these foods are high in fat and can raise blood cholesterol levels. Olive can be used sparingly.

Sugar:

This is a carbohydrate which provides energy but no vitamins, minerals or protein. Too much sugar can lead to weight gain.

Salt:

Salt or sodium chloride is found in many foods. Do not add more salt to food.

Thoughts and feelings

I have to tell you some instances to make you discern the meaning of thoughts and feelings.

Two people participated in a race. One got first prize and the other secured second prize. The former one practiced well before taking part in the race. The other must feel bad for his defeat. But this should be temporary. One must work very hard. If his feeling of defeat continues, it becomes stress. Some parents think of their children for a long time. This becomes a worry to them. This becomes stress. Stress leads to malady and malady to peace less life.

WEEK WISE COURSE

First Two Weeks:-

Sr.no.	Name of Asana	Duration per time	No. of times
1.	Padmasanam	2 minutes	1
2.	Pavanmukthasan	10 Seconds	3
3.	Uthi tha padasan	10 seconds	3
4.	Vibeeritha karani	5 Minutes	1
5.	Mathyasan	10 Seconds	3
6.	Vajrasan	2 minutes	2
7.	Mahamudhra	10 minutes	5
8.	Shanmukimudra	30 seconds	5
9.	Shanthi Asanam	10 minutes	1

Sr.no.	Name of Asana	Duration per time	No. of times
1.	Padmasana	2 minutes	1
2.	Vama yoga Mudra	10 seconds	3
3.	Pavanamuthasanam	10 seconds	3
4.	Janu Seerasan	10 seconds	3 (both Legs)
5.	Uthitha Padasanam	10 seconds	3

6.	Vibeeritha Karani	5 minutes	1
7.	Mathyasan	10 seconds	3
8.	Vajrasan	2 minutes	2
9.	Mahumudra	10 seconds	5
10.	Shanmuki Mudra	2 minutes	2
11.	Shanthi Asan	10 minutes	1

Sr.no.	**Name of Asana**	**Duration per time**	**No. of times**
1.	Padmasana	2 minutes	1
2.	Vama yoga Mudra	10 seconds	2
3.	Pavanamukthasanam	10 seconds	2 (both Legs)
4.	Janu Seerasan	10 seconds	2 (both Legs)
5.	Patchi Mothasan	5 seconds	3
6.	Uthitha Padasan	10 seconds	3
7.	Vibeeritha Karani	5 minutes	1
8.	Sarvangasan	2 minutes	2
9.	Halasan	10 seconds	2
10.	Mathyasan	10 seconds	2

11.	Vajrasan	2 minutes	2
12.	Mahumudra	10 seconds	2
13.	Shanmuki Mudra	2 minutes	2
14.	Shanthi Asan	5 minutes	1

Sr.no.	Name of Asana	Duration per time	No. of times
1.	Padmasana	2 minutes	1
2.	Yoga Mudra	10 seconds	2
3.	Pavanamukthasanam	10 seconds	2
4.	Janu Seerasan	10 seconds	2
5.	Patchi Mothasan	10 seconds	3
6.	Uthitha Padasanam	10 seconds	2
7.	Vibeeritha Karani	5 minutes	1
8.	Sarvangasan	3 minutes	2
9.	Halasan	10 seconds	1
10.	Mathyasan	10 seconds	2
11.	Bhujangasan	10 seconds	2
12.	Vajrasan	10 seconds	2
13.	Mahumudra	10 seconds	2

14.	Shanmuki Mudra	2 minutes	2
15.	Artha Sirasasanam	30 seconds	2
16.	Nindra Padasanam	10 seconds	2
17.	Marjari Asana	Up & down	5
18.	Pavana Muthasanam	10 (Rolling)	5
19.	Thratak	10 seconds	5
20.	Shanthi Asan	5 minutes	1

Sr.no.	Name of Asana	Duration per time	No. of times
1.	Bhujangasan	10 seconds	2
2.	Dhanurasan	10 seconds	2
3.	Salabasan	10 seconds	2
4.	Vajrasan	10 seconds	2
5.	Mahumudra	10 seconds	2
6.	Shanmuki Mudra	2 minutes	2
7.	Artha Sirasasan	30 seconds	2
8.	Nindra Padasan	30 seconds	2 (both legs)
9.	Marjari Asana	Up & down	5
10.	Pavana Muthasan	10 (Rolling)	5

11.	Thratak	10 seconds	5
12.	Shanthi Asan	5 minutes	5

Pranayamam (Breathing Exercise)

First Two Weeks:

No.	Name of Asana	Duration	Duration Puraka Duration Rechaka	
			Inhaling	**Exhaling**
1.	Suryakalai	5 times	5 seconds	10 seconds
2.	Chandrakalai	5 times	5 seconds	10 seconds

First Two Weeks:

1.	Suryakalai	7 times	7 seconds	14 seconds
2.	Chandrakalai	7 times	7 seconds	14 seconds
3.	Kapalbhati	10 times		

Third Two Weeks:

1. Suryakalai	10 times	7 seconds	14 seconds
2. Chandrakalai	10 times	7 seconds	14 seconds
3. Kapalbhati	10 times		

Fourth Two Weeks:

1.	Suryakalai	10 times	7 seconds	14 seconds
2.	Chandrakalai	10 times	7 seconds	14 seconds
3.	Nadisuthi	5 times	5 seconds	10 seconds
4.	Kapalbhati	10 times		

Fifth Two Weeks

1.	Suryakalai	10 times	7 seconds	14 seconds
2.	Chandrakalai	10 times	7 seconds	14 seconds
3.	Nadisuthi	5 times	5 seconds	10 seconds
4.	Kapalbhati	10 times		

AAM CHANTING AND STRESS BUSTER

Listening to internal music the best healer while one with more depression or anxiety, he/she could close eyes and should inhale and has to chant "Aah, ...Aah.... and Aahn or oh... oh.... ohm.

On chanting, our inner voice became still and calm. Generating positive vibration in the premises would keep thoughts flow rhythmically.

After finishing work, working people, can practice this for two months.

Long time practice, ie., more than two months, some aura would creative around the person. It would protect him from any mental illness.

There is no specific time to practice. Whenever, the time available one could chant.

Our true nature is blissful. Everyone wants to be happy. That is possible through. Aum (om) chanting. Our negative feelings like anger, fear, anxiety, stress, hatred will go away while chanting Om.

When we start chanting Om, it creates positive vibrations.

It purifies Aura.

It gives peace and calm. Looking energetic and younger.

It improves concentration and focus up on our work.

BRAIN WAVES AND OM CHANTING

Brain waves represent the electrical activity of the 100 billion neurons with in the brain. This electrical activity shows in waves of different frequencies in different state of consciousness.

The four main frequencies

1. Beta

2. Alpha

3. Theta and

4. Delta

1. Beta (14-40Hz)

The waking consciousness and reasoning wave. Beta waves ranging from 13 to 30 Hertz. When we all alert with physical world working, driving, talking etc. When the brains pulses in higher frequency, they are also rather weak, and shallow aptitude.

Those who suffer attention deficit disorder shows too little Beta in their EEG.

2. Alpha (75.-14Hz)

In this state consciously aware but not focused on the external world. It is possible to enter Alpha state if you stare at a thing for longer time (Candle meditation).

Chanting for 20 minutes, take to this level. Allowing your brain to slow down to alpha. Energy is restored. Repair and self-healing.

3. Theta (4.7 to 5Hz)

These waves state of importance for emotional healing through dreaming. It paves way for creativity, intuition and problem solving abilities of the sub-consciousness mind.

4. Delta (0.5 to 4Hz)

Delta belongs to deep dreamless sleep. This is essential for emotional and physical restoration. It is for anti-aging, growth hormones and encourage DNA repair. Here emotional imbalances Aare cured. And long term memory is enhanced.

Ganna (above 40 Hz) - (ESTACY)

(Extra Ordinary states of mind)

These waves occurs while brain functions at a very high level of synthesis, perceptions or memories into a greater, holistic understanding. It is the extreme level of insight, psychic talents. This happens for monks and yogis.

Mood swings, depression, anxiety and stress

In my experience, depression related problems, mood swings, anxiety all because of lack of prana in brain. The unknown prana is instilled through simple Pranayama, such as Kapala bhathi and Aloma and Viloma. In these practice, the person's attention hold on. And trained to or practiced to focus upon internal happy.

Unfortunately, now a days younger generation fall pray to such kind of problems.

Until 20 years back, depression would affect the old people. Recent studies and experience demonstrates that in childhood stage, all should have played well in the ground. And peer group activities, mingling with others lead to happier life in later days.

In this regard, person should have felt happiness in activities which stimulates all system in the body. Frequent Mood swings lead to damage the brain and physical body.

Stress and Brain

Chronic stress can damage brain structure and connectivity. Chronic stress and high levels of cortisol create long - lasting brain changes.

Young people, who one exposed to chronic stress early in life and prone to mental problems.

The gray matter of the brain densely packed nerve cell bodies and that is responsible for the brain's higher functions such as thinking and decision making. Gray matter is only half of the brain matter inside our heads, the half of brain volume is called white matha.

White Matha is comprised of axons, create network of fibnes that connect, neurons and creates a communications network between brain regions - and speeds the flow of electrical signals between neurons and brain regions.

White Matha is changing while Schizophrenia, autism, depression suicide.

The hippo campus regulates memory and emotions and plays a role in various emotional disorders and shrink after extended period of acute stress.

Regular physical activity and meditation are two effective ways to reduce stress and lower cortisol can improve brain structure and connectivity.

Optimism and anxiety change the brain structure

The OFC (Orbitofrontal Cortex) is a region, plays a role in anxiety disorders. The plays a central role in emotional and behavioral regulations by integrating intellectual and emotional information. The size of OFC predict his / her susceptibility to anxiety or propensity for optimism.

The thicker OFC on the left side of the brain corresponded to higher optimism and less anxiety. Optimism played a mediating role in reducing anxiety.

Sleep and its duration

While we think about sleep, we should concentrate upon timing. How long we sleep a day? How we sleep?

First of all, duration plays viral role, but at the same time, it should be very sound. Some people sleep for light hours, but on wake up, they would near fell freshness internally. It means physical body slept. But inner and sub conscious mind did not take rest. For this kind of problems, we should practice simple meditation or Pranayama.

When we have disturbed sleep. Our metabolism changed. Inside our body, some type of chemicals should be changed into other. That is regular. If not done properly. The organs gets no Prana - paring way for malfunction. It occurs not in a day, but over the years.

In later days, doctors would be unable to find out the reason for chemicals malfunction. Besides, we cannot prove that sleep. Sometimes, they would be awake for whole the right itself. The day after, two person would feel .... in his both eyes. The body would be trying to push out the heat through eyes. Total becomes uneasy.

Depression and Countries

I am not solo, but made up of flesh of social, political, economic push up

India is most vulnerable to depression. Led to mental health problems. Development fixes the civilians in constant stress and anxiety. More than 12 hours in the private companies led to this state.

Depression is under diagnosed and not treated at all - To the point there are 300 million depressed people in the world.

We think that the world has improved leaps and bounds in the last century. Technology has played a crucial role in this. Technology has made life easier. You can now exchange messages with loved ones thousands of miles away in the blink of an eyes. And so, technology has increased competition and pressure in the manner that has seen suicide rates steadily increase each year.

The one thing that order generation had and we are deprived of is, peace of mind no longer exists. And it is never enough.

Europe, which is considered to be one of the advanced continents in the world, has also seen a lot of depression in recent years.

In Europe, Ukraine is the most depressed state.

You may notice that the rich countries bend to have higher anxiety rates than poor ones.

While improvements have been made in the diagnosis of depression. Mental illness is synonymous with depression. USA has the most mental illness in the world.

Most depressed countries are:

10. Italy - 3.8 %

Reasons: death, divorce, school money - struggling political and economic environment.

9. Mexico - 4.8%

More women than men - (Single woman, divorced or windowed) - Families with traditional values plays vital role in decrease the divorce rate.

8. Spain - 4.9%

In Spain, Economic depression was bad. It lead to emotional distress as unemployment rates in soar. Adolescents one greatly affected by depression. Usage of antidepressant prescription is on high.

7. Belgium - 6.2%

Euthanization is major cause for depression in this country. Euthanization is legally approved for terminally ill children.

Naturally Euthanasia is a dangerous thing to a developed country. Cancer patients' request for euthanasia is on the rise.

6. Lebanon:

People, here, feel insecurity in their economy. It leads to usage anti-depressant prescriptions along with sedatives and sleeping pills.

People worry about future of their homes, jobs and families. Citizen prefer medications our therapy.

5. Columbia - 6.8%

   Political hardship, war and economic downturn.

4. Netherlands - 6.9%

   Dutch culture more morose than that of their neighbors. A lot depends on individual context.

3. France - 8.5%

   People suffer from clinical depression, the French often wearing black, drinking coffee or wine, all the fue while smoking, all in cynical manner. Citizen of France consume more anti-depressants than any other world.

2. Ukraine - 9.1%

   Tensions are high in the Ukraine. Depression is considered to be the western illness. Political system has not helped to retrieve from it.

Stress Hormone - Cortisol.

The Primary Stress Hormone

Adrenaline increase our heart rate, elevates our blood pressure and boosts energy supplies.

Cortisol, the primary stress hormone increases sugars in the blood stream, enhances your brains' use of glucose and increases the availability of substances that repair tissues.

During stress message is sent to the part of the brain called hypothalamus, which releases Corticotrophin - releasing hormone (CRH) - CRH then tells the pituitary gland to release adrenocorticotropic hormone - which tells the adrenal glands to produce cortisol.

Besides, very accurately mention, the stress hormones - when stress sets off the usual ferocious communication between the hypothalamus and the pituitary, the buek stops at the adrenal glands. They manufacture and release the true stress hormones - dopamine, epinephrine (also known as adrenaline), norepinephrine (Nora adrenaline) and especially cortisol.

In addition, in response to stress extra cortisol is released to help the body to respond appropriately.

In women, high cortisol levels contribute to changes in woman's libido and menstrual cycle. Anxiety depression may also be linked to high cortisol levels. At the sometime low cortisol levels can cause a condition known as primary adrenal insufficiency.

If stress hormones are too low, muscles have insufficient fuel and oxygen to respond quickly, however excessive secretion of stress hormones can disturb the balance between fat and carbohydrate metabolism and damage physical performance with inflammation.

Public Health Enemy:

High levels of cortisol interfere with learning and memory, lower immune function and bone density, increase weight gain, blood pressure, cholesterol level and heart disease.

Besides, it increases the risk for depression, mental illness and lower life expectancy. It is a potential trigger for mental illness and decreased resistance - especially in adolescence.

There are two types of stress: 1) Eustress 2) distress.

Eustress is good stress.

Both eustress and distress release cortisol part of the general adaptation syndrome.

The cortisol awakening (CAR) response is represented by a typical 50 percent increase of cortisol levels that occur 20 to 80 minutes after waking up in the morning.

CAR is typically less active on days off and weekends resulting in lower morning cortisol levels.

But one reason that people ages 65 - 90 may have lower cortisol levels in the morning might be linked to someone being retired to or not feeling a need to seize of the day.

Reduce your cortisol naturally

1. Oil Bath
2. Sleep - viparita karani - Mudra
3. Breathing Exercise – Kapala bhathi

Kapala bhathi and reducing Cortisol

'Kapala' means 'head' (or) 'brain' - 'bhathi' means "pure"

With stress, our brain has accumulated with stress, our brain has accumulated with stress and unwanted thoughts. When we are afflicted with mental strain or continuous repeated thoughts. Our system internally began to damage itself.

It means absence of prana or reducing the level of prana - it many happen little by little day by day. Sometimes sudden breakdown of prana charge in brain would lead to complex state of hormones in the body.

Perhaps, in brain is master gland pituitary which and could be activated only by prana. Master gland controls the system. Initially it should be charged. And then automatically adrenaline won't be affected.

Not only stress, any disease may be, your head in very important thing. In yoga, we call it thind eye or powerful energy center or 'Ajna' chakra.

Head is the king of all parts of body. When it became very active, all other parts would be very active. Our body's entire control is in the brain.

Now let us see procedure of 'Kapala bhathi' - sit any posture, close your mouth, exhale through nose forcibly - ie. - Exhale quickly - should not inhale voluntarily. Three times at a stretch. As usual, let in allow breath. This is a cycle. It should be done for thirty times. In the beginning, practice for ten times. And after a week, fifteen times. And then add fine times.

While practicing this, some vacuum occur in the brain. Now, more prana would be let in naturally. While repeating it for twenty times, the pituitary becomes much energized. Secretion of cortisol automatically come down.

Oil bath

Oil bath is the best technique to relax the body muscle and internal system.

It improves the general body health. In ancient yogi, Theraiyar in Tamil, he advised us to take oil bath twice a week.

It tones up muscle. And regulates all endocrine glands, so stress will be off. It gives us sound sleep.

Method

Take gingelly oil or coconut oil. 300 ml in a boul. put in some garlic, cumin in it. Boil it for ten minutes. Apply it over the body. All parts of body should be applied. You should wait for 40 minutes and take bath in warm water. For clean it use natural herbal powder. On that day, you will be feeling sleepy. But should not sleep.

Body is unwanted temperature will be down. Both cold and heat would be balanced.

Unwanted heat is major the reason for damage of endocrine system. Oil bath improves longevity.

Natural Food

To reduce stress, food is very important. Without right food one cannot live healthy.

There are three types of food in Indian Philosophy. 1. Tano 2. Rajo 3. Satva

Natural - Diet Plan

Morning:

1. Upon Wake up - 300ml water - ½ lemon, two spoon honey - mixed together drink.

2. 7.00 a.m. - Asanas and Pranayams.

3. 8.00 a.m. - Breakfast 1. Sprows, Moon dal, Fenugreek, Ground Nut

4. 11.00 a.m. - Raw vegetable juice

5. 2.00 p.m. - Lunch - Rice + 2 green vegetables (half boiled)

6. 7.00 p.m. - All fruits (As much as possible)

Before sleeping Om Chanting.

NATURAL FOOD FOR DEPRESSION

RAW DIET AND ITS PREPARATION

1. Synopsis

Fresh or raw diet has many advantages especially in illness and is the best Protection against diseases. Raw fruits and vegetables are an ideal food, very high in food value. They contain the vitamins and minerals required by the body in their natural state apart from their healing properties. Fruits and uncooked vegetables are solvents. Their juices dissolve foreign matter in the blood and make it ready for elimination from the system; hence they are effective in restoring the body to health. While raw fruits are the cleaners of the body due to high carbon content, raw vegetables are the builders of the cells and tissues of the body apart from their value as cleaners and regenerators of the liver and kidneys.

During the period of eating raw food, there may appear symptoms of flatulence, intestinal pains, headache, and general debility and so on. All these are processes of purification and healing. The fresh or raw diet serves as an aid in combating intestinal toxemia, constipation, obesity, chronic diseases and illness.

Hence as a whole, the raw food diet is said to detoxify the system, improve vitality and help people to lose weight.

2. Super Salad (With Honey Dressing)

Serves: 2

Calories: 85 Cal

Ingredients: 50gms (1 .75 oz) carrot; 20gms (0.70 oz) bell pepper; 30gms (1.05 oz) pine-apple; 10gms (0.35oz) honey; salt and black pepper powder a pinch.

Method: Chop the carrot, bell pepper and pine-apple into thin strips of equal shape and size. Dress with honey, salt and pepper mixture and serve.

Importance: Specially recommended for patients with obesity and eye disorders.

3. Orchards (with lemon honey dressing)

Serves: 2

Calories: 94 cal

Ingredients: 50gms (1.75 oz) apple; 25gms (0.88 oz) kohlrabi; 25gms (0.88 oz) green grapes; 10gms (0.35 oz) honey; "lOgms (0.35 oz) lemon juice; 2gms green chilies (small green whole peppers).

Method: Grate kohlrabi. Halve the grapes and remove the seeds. Cut the apple into small pieces. Cut green chilies into pieces. Beat honey and lemon juice. Add to it the finely cut green chilies and blend all well. Mix the dressing with the salad and serve immediately.

Importance: Mainly recommended for obese and hypertensive patients.

Can also be served to diabetics (honey excluded).

4. Cucumber Paradise (with banana dressing)

Serves: 4

Calories: 205 cal

Ingredients: 75gms (2.65 oz) cucumber; 25gms (0.88 oz) bell pepper; 50gms (1.75 oz) carrot; 25gms (0.88 oz) ripe banana; 75ml (0.13 pint) milk; 75ml (0.13 pint) water; 20gms (0.70oz) brown sugar (jaggery).

Method: Chop cucumber, bell pepper and carrots into small pieces. Blend banana, milk, water and jaggery. Mix all the ingredients thoroughly and serve cold.

Importance: Generally recommended for hypertensive patients.

5. Cabbage Kosambari (with seasoning)

Serves: 2

Calories: 167 cal

Ingredients: 100gms (3.5 oz) cabbage; 20gms (0.70 oz) grated coconut; 5gms (0.18oz) green chilies; 15gms (0.53 oz) lemon juice; 20gms (0.70 oz) coriander leaves; 5gms (0.18 oz) mustard seeds; 5gms (0.18 oz) oil; a pinch of asafetida; salt as per taste.

Method: Chop the raw cabbage, green chilies and coriander leaves very finely. Heat oil and add the mustard seeds. Let it splutter. Then add the green chilies and asafetida. Fry well till the aroma comes. To the chopped cabbage, add grated coconut, coriander leaves, salt and lemon juice. Season it and mix thoroughly. Serve immediately.

Importance: Specially recommended for diabetic, obese, anemic, fracture cases and also patients with ulcer in the stomach and duodenum.

6. Carrot Trupti (with avocado dressing)

Serves: 2

Calories: 75 cal

Ingredients: 50gms (1.75oz) carrot; 25gms (0.88oz) avocado; 10gms (0.35 oz) honey.

Method: Chop the carrots finely. Make a dressing by blending the avocado (remove seeds) with honey. Mix the dressing with chopped carrot and serve.

Importance: To be avoided by diabetic and obese patients. Recommended For hypertension and other diseases.

Cucumber Crimson (with passion fruit/orange dressing)

Serves: 2

Calories: 55 cal

Ingredients: 50gms (1.75 oz) cucumber; 50gms (1.75 oz) carrot; 50gms (1.75 oz) passion fruit pulp/orange; salt and black pepper powder as per taste.

Method: Chop carrots and cucumber into small pieces. Blend passion fruit pulp with salt and pepper powder. If passion fruit is not available, then chop the oranges into small pieces with skin and seeds removed. Mix all together well. Serve cold.

Importance: The salad is recommended for obese and hypertensive patients (salt excluded from the salad).

8. Carrot Salad

Serves: 2

Calories: 265 cal

Ingredients: 100gms (3.5 oz) carrot; 50gms (1.75 oz) apple; 25gms (0.88 oz) peanuts; 1tsp honey; 1tsp lemon juice; 75ml (0.13 pint) yogurt.

Method: Shred the carrot into thin, long, thread like strips. Cut the apple into small cubes. Roast the groundnut and powder it coarsely. Mix well all the ingredients. Serve immediately.

Importance: To be excluded by diabetics. Good for obesity and eye related problems.

9. Kohlrabi Salad

Serves: 2

Calories: 195 cal

Ingredients: 100gms (3.5 oz) kohlrabi; 25gms (0.88 oz) whole green gram sprouts; 25gms (0.88 oz) bell pepper; 50gms (1.75 oz) carrot; 25gms (0.88 oz) pomegranate seeds; 2tbsp french dressing (salad oil, honey, lemon juice. All mixed together); carrot leaves to garnish.

Method: Shred kohlrabi, bell pepper and carrot into thin long strips. Mix pomegranate and gram sprouts to the shredded vegetables. Mix all with the trench dressing. Shred the carrot leaves and garnish on top.

Importance: The above salad is recommended for hypertensive, obese and diabetic patients (carrot excluded).

10. Creamy Sprouted Moong Salad

Serves: 4

Calories: 320 cal

Ingredients: 250gms (8.83 oz) skimmed yoghurt; 50gms (1.75 oz) french beans; 20gms (0.07oz) green gram sprouts; 10gms (0.35 oz) chopped coriander leaves; 1/2 tsp roasted cumin powder; 100gms (3.5 oz) cucumber: 40gms (1.41 oz) tomato; 5gms (0.18 oz) green chilies chopped; 50gms (1.75 oz) potato; 10gms (0.35 oz) lemon juice; black pepper powder and honey as per taste.

Method: Wash and chop the trench beans, cucumber, tomato and potato. Parboil the trench beans and potato. Mix all the vegetables and other ingredients and serve.

Importance: The salad is prescribed for diabetic, obese and hypertensive patients especially.

11. Plantain Pith (banana tree stem) Salad

Serves: 2

Calories: 212 cal

Ingredients: 25gms (0.88 oz) plantain pith; 25gms (0.88 oz) green gram sprouts; 10gms (0.35 oz) coconut; 5gms (0.18 oz) oil; 5gms(0.18oz) mustard seeds; 1 lemon; 75ml (0.13 pint) yogurt; a pinch of asafetida; a pinch of salt.

Method: Cut the plantain pith into small thin squares and remove fiber. Grate coconut. Mix all the above ingredients. Season it with the seasoning. Squeeze lemon, mix and serve.

Importance: This salad helps to postpone the age and also recommended for Diabetic, obese and hypertensive patients (salt excluded). Patients with kidney stones, gastric and stomach ulcers also benefits by the intake of this salad.

2 Exotic Fruity Salad

Serves: 2

Calories: 240 cal

Ingredients: 50gms (1.75 oz) orange; 200gms (7oz) ripe papaya; 50gms (1.75 oz) pineapple; 50gms (1.75 oz) whole green gram sprouts, 1 tsp vinegar; 50gms (1.75oz) cucumber; 2tsp salad oil; salt and black pepper powder as per taste, a few mint leaves grinded to a paste.

Method: Cut the orange into small pieces and remove the fiber and seeds. De-skin the papaya, pineapple and cucumber. Chop these fruits into small cubes. Mix all the cut fruits and vegetables and add the remaining ingredients. Again mix well. Serve immediately.

Importance: This salad is useful in cases of diabetes, obesity, and hypertension. Also serves as an all-purpose general salad.

Moong and Cucumber Salad

Serves: 1

Calories: 80 cal.

Ingredients: 15gms (0.53 oz) green gram sprouts; 20gms (0.88 oz) cucumber; 15gms (0.53 oz) parboiled potatoes; 1/4tsp salad oil; 1/4tsp vinegar; 1tsp milk; 10gms (0.35 oz) lettuce; 50gms (1.75 oz) carrot; a pinch of black pepper powder; salt as per taste.

Method; Chop the cucumber, parboiled potatoes and carrot into small pieces. And rest of the ingredients and mix well. Garnish with chopped lettuce leaves.

Importance: Can be prescribed for obese and hypertensive patients (salt excluded).

14. Corn/ Moong Apple Salad

Serves: 4

Calories: 410 cal/serving.

Ingredients: 10Qgms (3.5 oz) cucumber; 100gms (3.5 oz) apple; 200gms (7 oz) parboiled potatoes; 10gms (0.35 oz) lettuce; 10gms (0.35 oz) mustard powder; 2tsp lemon juice; 50gms (1.75 oz) apple juice; 5tsp salad oil; salt and black pepper powder as per taste; 20gms (0.88oz) corn cobs.

Method: Chop the cucumber, parboiled potatoes and apple into small cubes add the rest of the ingredients and mix well. Garnish with chopped lettuce leaves.

Importance: Especially beneficial for obese and hypertensive patients.

15. Summer Retreat

Serves: 1

Calories: 150 cal

Ingredients: 100gms (3.5 oz) cucumber; 100gms (3.5 oz) tomatoes; 1 lemon; 1/2 coconut; a few coriander leaves; salt as per taste.

Method: Chop the cucumber and tomatoes into small cubes. Grate coconut and add to the chopped vegetables. Squeeze lemon and salt into it. Mix well and garnish with chopped coriander leaves.

Importance: The salad is refreshing during the hot summer months. As a diet, this salad can be prescribed to diabetic, obese (coconut excluded) and hypertensive patients (salt excluded).

16. Raw Papaya Salad

Serves: 3

Calories: 90 cal/serving

Ingredients: 100gms ((3.5 oz) carrot; 100gms (3.5 oz) raw papaya; 100gms (3.5oz) guava; a small bunch of chopped coriander leaves; 1 lemon; 2tsp salad oil; salt and black pepper powder to taste.

Method: Grate the carrot and the papaya. Chop the guava (seeds removed) into small cubes. Squeeze the lemon into the chopped ingredients and add the remaining items. Mix well and garnish with chopped coriander leaves. Serve.

Importance: Can be served to obese and hypertensive patients (salt excluded)

17. Guava Delight

Serves: 1

Calories: 55 cal

Ingredients: 50gms (1.75 oz) guava; 25gms (0.88 oz) pine-apple; 5gms (0.18 oz) mint; salt and black pepper powder to taste.

Method: Chop the pine-apple and the guava (seeds removed) into thin long strips. Mix well with finely chopped mint leaves, salt and black pepper powder.

Serve.

Importance: This is a delicious fruit salad in general and can also be prescribed to diabetic, obese and hypertensive patients (salt excluded).

18. Summer's Salad

Serves: 1

Calories: 50 cal

Ingredients: 50gms (1 .75 oz) carrot; 20gms (0.88 oz) cucumber; 5gms (0.18 oz) bell pepper; 50gms (1 .05 oz) apple;

1 0gms (0.35 oz) orange; 5gms (0.18 oz) raisins; a few coriander leaves; salt and black pepper powder to taste.

Method: Chop cucumber, bell pepper and apple into small cubes. Remove re skin and seeds from orange and cut into small pieces. Grate the carrot. Add raisins, chopped coriander leaves; salt and black pepper powder as per taste. Mix well and serve.

Importance: This salad is beneficial for obese/overweight people. The fruits and vegetables which make up this salad have weight reducing properties and hence consumption, helps to slim down.

19. Melon and Pineapple Salad

Serves: 2

Calories: 125 cal

Ingredients: 250gms (8.82 oz) water-melon; 100gms (3.5 oz) pineapple; 2tsp honey; a few finely chopped fresh mint leaves; 3tsp roasted cumin powder.

Method: Cut the water-melon (seeds removed) and pineapple into small pieces. Mix well with honey and chopped mint leaves. Serve immediately.

Importance: A general purpose fruit salad which can be especially recommended to diabetic, obese and hypertensive patients.

20. Grated Salad

Serves: 1

Calories: 85 cal

Ingredients: 25gms (0.88 oz) cucumber; 50gms (1.75 oz) beetroot; 50gms (1.75 oz) carrot; 1 lemon; 1/2tsp roasted cumin powder; salt and black pepper powder to taste.

Method: Scrape off the skin of cucumber, beetroot ad carrot. Chop cucumber into small cubes. Grate carrot and beetroot. Mix the entire salad thoroughly with lemon juice, salt, black pepper powder and cumin powder. Serve.

Importance: Recommended for obese patients.

21. Cabbage and Pineapple Salad

Serve: 2

Calories: 110 cal

Ingredients: 100gms (3.5 oz) cabbage; 15gms (0.53 oz) pineapple; 15gms (0.53 oz) lettuce; 25gms (0.88 oz) green bell pepper; 75gms (2.65 oz) red beetroot; salt and black pepper powder as per taste; 1tsp honey; 1 lemon.

Method: Grate cabbage and beetroot. Chop pineapple and bell pepper into small cubes. Add salt, black pepper powder, honey, lemon juice to the cut fruits and vegetables. Mix well and serve.

Importance: The salad is beneficial in cases of diabetes, acidity and ulcers, anemia and for patients with low calcium level, bone fractures etc.

22. Fruit and Vegetable Salad

Serves: 2

Calories: 275 cal

Ingredients: 10Ogms (3.5 oz) beetroot; 50gms (1.75 oz) cucumber; 50gms (1.75 oz) potato; 50gms (1.75 oz) carrot: 10Ogms (3.5 oz) chopped pineapple; 50gms (1.75'oz) apple; 125ml (0.22 pint) yogurt; 15gms (0.88 oz) lettuce; salt as per taste; roasted coriander and cumin powder.

Method: Parboil the potato. Chop beetroot, carrot, cucumber, Potato. Mix the entire salad with diced apple, pineapple, curds, chopped lettuce, salt, roasted coriander and cumin powder. The fruit and vegetable salad is now ready to be served.

Importance: Obese patients can take this salad.

23: Curd Delight

Serves: 2

Calories: 260 cal

Ingredients: 200ml (0.5 pint) thick skimmed yogurt; 50gms (1.75 oz) grated red beetroot; 100gms *(3.5* oz) grated carrot; 1/4 cup spinach (cut and blanched); 1 tbsp finely chopped mint leaves; 6tsp sugar (optional); 1tsp roasted cumin powder;

100gms (3.5 oz) potato boiled and cut into pieces; 50gms (1.75 oz) grated cucumber; a pinch of salt.

Method: Mix all the ingredients. Serve at normal temperature or chilled.

Importance: A delicious salad when served chilled during the hot summer months. Also recommended for obesity.

24. Vegetable Pachadi

Serves: 2

Calories: 100 cal

Ingredients: 50gms (1.75 oz) cucumber; 50gms (1.75 oz) tomato; 50gms (1.75 oz) onion; 10gms 0.35 oz) ginger; 10gms (0.35 oz) chopped coriander leaves; 1 green chili; 1tsp mustard seeds; 10gms (0.35 oz) oil; 10gms (0.35 oz) curry leaves; salt as per taste; 250ml (0.44 pint) thick skimmed buttermilk; 1tsp roasted cumin powder.

Method: Grate the cucumber. Chop the tomato and onion into small pieces. Grate ginger and green chilly. Mix the cucumber, tomato, onion with buttermilk. Heat oil. Add the mustard seeds. When it splutters, add the curry leaves and ginger. Fry for a minute and then add it to the pachadi (grated and chopped vegetables). Mix with salt, roasted cumin powder according to taste. Garnish with chopped coriander leaves and grated chili.

Importance: A cool, soothing and refreshing salad which can be recommended for diabetic, obese and hypertensive patients (salt excluded).

25. Cucumber Re-mix

Serves: 2

Calories: 116 cal

Ingredients: 100gms (3.5 oz) cucumber; 50gms (1.75 oz) apple; 50gms (1.75 oz) orange; 50gms (1.75 oz) water-melon; 10Ogms (3.5 oz) raw papaya; 1 lemon; 1tsp roasted cumin powder; salt and black pepper powder as per taste.

Method: De-skin the cucumber. Chop the cucumber, apple, orange and water-melon into small cubes. Grate the raw papaya. Squeeze lemon into the salad. Add a pinch of salt, roasted cumin powder and black pepper powder.

Mix well and serve soon.

Importance: This is a general purpose salad. Obese, diabetics, hypertensive and constipative patients find this salad to be beneficial. It contains a high amount of fiber.

26. Russian salad

Serves: 1

Calories: 104 cal

Ingredients: 50gms (1.75 oz) double beans (chopped and parboiled); 50gms (1.75 oz) carrot diced; 25gms (0.88 oz) apple chopped; 25gms (0.88 oz) pineapple chopped; 50gms (1.75 oz) cucumber diced; a pinch of black pepper powder; a few chopped coriander leaves; salt as per taste.

Method: Mix all the fruits and vegetables. Add black pepper powder and salt; and toss well. Garnish with chopped coriander leaves.

Importance: The salad proves to be beneficial in cases of constipation, obesity and hypertension (salt excluded).

27. Fruit Chart

Serves: 2

Calories: 112 cal

Ingredients: 15gms ((0.53 oz) ripe banana; 50gms (1.05 oz) boiled potato; 50gms (1.05 oz) boiled sweet potato; 15gms (0.53 oz) guava; 10gms (0.35 oz) grape fruit; 5gms (0.18 oz) lemon juice; 2gms (0.07 oz) red chili powder; 2gms (0.07 oz) raw mango powder; 1 gms (0.04 oz) roasted cumin powder; 2gms (0.07 oz) sugar (optional); salt as per taste.

Method: All the fruits are cut into small pieces and mixed the above spices including lemon juice as required. This mixture called chart is now ready and should be served soon.

Importance: This is a general fruit salad. It can be served to hypertensive patients (salt excluded) but to be avoided by diabetics and obese.

28. Tri Colored Salad

Serves: 2

Calories: 31 cal

Ingredients: 100gms (3.5 oz) orange; 100gms (3.5 oz) apple; 100gms (3.*5 oz)* ripe papaya or water-melon; 100gms (3.5 oz) cucumber; 2tsp roasted r.min powder; 1 tsp salad oil; a pinch of salt; 15gms (0.53 oz) chopped coriander leaves; 20gms (0.88 oz) roasted peanut powder.

Method: De-skin the oranges, papaya and cucumber. Chop these and the apples into small cubes. Mix with roasted cumin powder, salad oil, salt and chopped coriander leaves. Sprinkle roasted peanut powder and serve immediately.

Importance: Suitable for diabetes, obcsity, hypertension (salt excluded) *and* in constipation.

29. Fruit Curd Shake

Serves: 2

Calories: 248 cal.

Ingredients: 250ml (0.44 pint) thick skimmed yogurt; 250ml (0.44 pint) thick juice of ripe papaya or avocado; 20gms (0.88 oz) de-skinned chopped oranges; 20gms (0.88 oz) water-melon; 20gms (0.88oz) pears; 20gms (0.88oz) chopped apple; 10gms (0.35 oz) pomegranate seeds; 10gms (0.35oz) guava/pineapple; 5 gms (0.18 oz) cardamom powder; 1 0gms (0.35oz) roasted cashew nuts.

Method: Blend well the yogurt and the papaya juice in the blender. Mix this with all the chopped fruits. Sprinkle the roasted cashew nut powder and cardamom powder. Serve the fruit curd shake chilled.

Importance: This is a tasty salad and can be safely given to diabetic and *obese* patients. Fruits such as avocado and pineapple may be added instead of ripe papaya and guava, when serving as a general purpose salad and not: o patients (diabetics and obese should abstain from avocado and pineapple).

30. Raw Vegetable Salad

Serves: 2

Calories: 260 cal

Ingredients: 400gms (14 oz) cabbage; 100gms (3.55 oz) carrot; 50gms (1.75 oz) red beetroot; 50gms (1.75 oz) ripe tomato; 2tsp salad oil; 1 tsp vinegar; 10gms (0.35 oz) chopped coriander leaves; salt and black pepper powder as per taste.

Method: Grate the cabbage, carrot and beet-root. Chop the tomato into small cubes and remove the seeds. Mix the grated and chopped vegetables with the remaining ingredients and serve.

Importance: The salad is good in cases of constipation, gastric ulcers, acidity, anemia, obesity and hypertension (salt excluded).

31. Beans and Cabbage Salad

Serves: 1

Calories: 75 cal

Ingredients: 10gms (0.35 oz) french beans; 10gms (0.35 oz) green gram sprouts; 15gms (0.53 oz) ripe tomato; 20gms (0.71 oz) cabbage; 10gms (0.35 oz) chopped coriander leaves; 5gms (0.18 oz) lemon juice/vinegar; 1tsp salad oil; salt and black pepper powder as per taste.

Method: Parboil the French beans. Chop the tomato into small cubes. Grate the cabbage. Mix well all the vegetables and other ingredients. Serve immediately.

Importance: Good for obesity, diabetes, gastric ulcers, acidity, constipation, hypertension (salt excluded).

32. Spinach Salad

Serves: 1

Calories: 40 cal

Ingredients: 5gms ((0.18 oz) tender spinach leaves; 5gms (0.18 oz) mushroom; 50gms (1.75 oz) cucumber; 20gms (0.88 oz) ripe tomato; 10gms (0.35 oz) carrot; 10gms (0.35 oz) lemon juice; salt and black pepper powder as per taste.

Method: Clean, chop and steam the mushrooms. Wash and grate the carrot. De-skin the cucumber and chop cucumber and tomato (seeds removed) into small round pieces. Wash and cut the spinach leaves into thin long strips. For serving arrange the grated coconut and mushroom in the center of the serving dish. Arrange the tomato and cucumber all around it. Sprinkle the salad with spinach leaves. Squeeze lemon, salt and black pepper powder all around the salad and serve.

Importance: Recommended for obesity, hypertension (salt excluded), eye disorders and constipation.

33. Summer Salad

Serves: 3

Calories: 225 cal

Ingredients: 180gms (6.35 oz) radish; 600gms (21 oz) cucumber; 10gms (0.35 oz) mushroom; 200gms (7 oz) ripe tomatoes; 30gms (1.06 oz) green bell pepper; 10gms (0.35 oz) lettuce; 10gms (0.35 *oz)* lemon juice; 2tsp salad oil; salt and black pepper powder as per taste.

Method: De-skin cucumber and radish. Cut radish and cucumber longitudinally into thin flat slices. Wash, chop and steam the mushrooms. Cut the tomato (seeds removed) and bell pepper into thin round slices. Chop the lettuce leaves. Mix all the vegetables well with lemon juice, salad oil, and salt and pepper powder. Sprinkle with lettuce leaves and serve.

Importance: Patients with obesity, hypertension (salt excluded), constipation, may be benefited from this raw salad. This is a refreshing salad with a satiety feeling during the hot summer months.

34. Cauliflower and Mushroom Salad

Serves: 1

Calories: 100 cal

Ingredients: 100gms (3.5 oz) cauliflower; 40gms (1.41 oz) mushroom; 25gms (0.88 oz) avocado, 2tsp yogurt; 1tsp chopped parsley.

Method: Wash and chop the cauliflower into small flowerets. Then, parboil it. Wash and chop the mushroom and steam it. Cut the avocado fruit into small pieces. Mix all well with beaten yogurt. Sprinkle the salad with chopped parsley leaves and serve.

Importance: This is a general salad and can also be served to diabetic and hypertensive patients.

35. Spinach Carrot Toss Salad

Serves: 1

Calories: 110 cal

Ingredients: 50gms (1.75 oz) spinach; 150gms (5.25 oz) carrot; 1 tsp lemon juice; 3/4 cup yoghurt; salt and black pepper powder to taste;

Method: Wash and thinly slice the carrot. Also wash and cut the spinach leaves into thread like strips. Mix the vegetables well with beaten yoghurt, lemon juice, salt and black pepper powder to taste and then serve.

Importance: Important in cases of obesity, hypertension (salt excluded), constipation, intestinal disorders (putrefaction, colitis).

36. Melon Kheer Salad

Serves: 1

Calories: 148 cal

Ingredients: 50gms (1.75 oz) muskmelon; 100gms (3.5 oz) water-melon; 100gms (3.5 oz) cucumber; 50gms (1.75 oz) carrot; 1 tbsp chopped coriander leaves; 1 tbsp honey; salt and black pepper powder as per taste.

Method: Chop the muskmelon, water-melon (seeds removed) and cucumber into small cubes. Grate the carrot. Make a dressing of honey, salt and pepper powder. Mix this with the salad. Serve with chopped coriander leaves sprinkled on top.

Importance: A refreshing salad for the hot summer months. The salad can be served to obese and hypertensive patients (salt excluded).

37. Bell pepper And Tomato Salad

Serves: 1

Calories: 68 cal

Ingredients: 10Ogms (3.5 oz) green bell pepper; 10Ogms (3.5 oz) ripe tomato; 1 tsp salad oil; 2tsp lemon juice; salt and pepper powder to taste. Method: Chop the capsicum and tomato (seeds removed) into thin long strips. Mix it with salad oil, lemon juice, salt and pepper powder. Serve immediately.

Importance: This salad may be served to diabetic, obese, hypertensive patients (salt excluded)

www.ingramcontent.com/pod-product-compliance
Lightning Source LLC
LaVergne TN
LVHW050316160826
845677LV00014B/3419

* 9 7 8 9 3 8 6 4 4 7 6 7 8 *